Benjamin Twos

by Derrick Browne

Trumps Publishing

Sydney Australia

Acknowledgements
Thanks to Lynn Lovelock, Leigh Browne, John de Ravin and Bruce Hovey for proofreading. Amongst the experts who gave their time to offer suggestions or views were John Roberts, Colleen Pidcock, Kieran Dyke, Peter Gill, George Jesner and Ron Klinger. Last but not least, it is a great honour to have a foreword by Albert Benjamin, the inventor of Benjamin Twos.

In memory of Wendy Browne

ISBN 0 9585266 1 3

First published 1993 by The Bridge Shop
2nd Edition November 1999 by Trumps Publishing
PO Box 939, Spit Junction 2088, Australia
Phone (02) 9969 5959

Typesetting by Nick Hughes

Artwork by Jason McDonald

Printed by McPherson's Printing Group

Foreword by Albert Benjamin

"This is the book I would like to have been able to write. Derrick has expounded my convention with much greater clarity than I could ever have achieved. The example hands of bidding and play are neat and to the point as are the quizzes.
"He has cast a strong light with simple logic to illuminate the finer points which bring maturity to the convention and will give confidence to every bridge player who will learn it and adapt it to his game. I am very grateful to Derrick Browne."

Albert Benjamin
September 1999

Introducing Benjamin Twos

Bidding can be obstructive or constructive. Three-level and higher openings, which wipe out several levels of bidding, aim mainly to obstruct the opponents' communication. One-level openings, on the other hand, do little to interfere with the opponents but leave room for us to find our best contract.

What of opening bids at the two-level? Any bidding system needs to include a way for opener, when superstrong, to force partner to speak. Two-level bids were logically assigned this role. However, such hands occur only rarely, whereas weak hands where a two-bid could obstruct the opponents' bidding are frequent.

In the mid-1950s, Scottish internationals Albert Benjamin and George Jesner found a way to combine both approaches to maximum advantage. Playing Benjamin Twos, opening bids of 2♥ or 2♠ are weak, forcing the opponents to start looking for a fit at a high level. The 2♣ and 2♦ openings, which would not be so useful as obstructive openings, are instead harnessed to show the powerhouse hands; they say nothing yet about suit, but keep the auction low enough for the suit to be shown comfortably on the next round.

If you are changing to Benjamin Twos after playing Strong Twos, you will find the weak twos in the majors are an exciting way to get into the auction more often.

If you are progressing from "weak twos and strong 2♣" you will discover that Benjamin Twos allow for better description of your strong hands, for the small loss of the weak 2♦ (which is of little pre-emptive value anyway).

Benjamin Twos are widely played in Australia, Britain, New Zealand and elsewhere, and French Standard features a similar structure. Benjamin Twos are interesting and challenging - enjoy them!

Derrick Browne
Sydney, November 1999

Contents

Benjamin Two openings at a glance

2♣   artificial, long suit
         & at least 8-9 playing tricks

2◇   artificial, about 23+ HCP
         or any game force

2♡/2♠   weak twos
         good 6-card suit, 6-10 HCP

2NT   balanced hand, 21-22 points

WEAK TWOS

Mini-preempts

Chapter 1
WEAK TWOS (2♡ & 2♠)

Weak twos are sometimes described as mini pre-empts. A weak two shows 6-10 HCP, just like a pre-emptive 3-opening. The difference is that a weak two shows a good 6-card suit, instead of the 7-card or longer suit expected for a higher level pre-empt.

A weak two gives partner a clear picture of opener's hand before the opponents get a word in.

Requirements

You should have

- 6-10 HCP

- good 6-card suit

> ♠ K Q 10 8 6 4
> ♡ K 8
> ♢ 9 7 5
> ♣ 3 2

The hand above is a classic weak two. Open 2♠.

It is preferable *not* to open a weak two with

- four cards in the other major

- a void

Any pre-emptive bid, including a weak two, makes it hard to find a fit in another suit which is why you should not have a 4-card major on the side.

A void may dramatically increase your playing strength if a good fit exists. So if you want a chance to assess how the hands fit, pass first or, with 10 HCP and a void, open one of the long suit.

♠ K J 9 8
♥ A Q 9 8 7 6
♦ —
♣ 9 5 4

Open 1♥. The void and the 4-card major both suggest a 1-opening may be better than a 2-opening on this 10 HCP hand. With the same shape but a weaker hand, pass first and await developments.

To open a weak two, prefer to have at least two honours in the long suit (Q10 xxxx or better). This is particularly the case when vulnerable:

♠ A 8 6 4 3 2
♥ K 5
♦ 9 8 2
♣ 8 2

If not vulnerable, a 2♠ opening on this hollow suit would be naughty but nice. Vulnerable, it would be just plain naughty.

♠ 3 2
♥ Q 10 8 7 5 4
♦ A 8 2
♣ 8 2

A 2♥ opening is standard on the hand above if not vulnerable. Even if vulnerable, 2♥ is reasonable, but this is a close decision.

With a 7-card suit, it is normal to open with a pre-emptive 3-opening, not a weak two. Rarely, the vulnerability may suggest it is wise to make an exception:

♠ A 10 9 5 4 3 2
♥ Q 5
♦ 9 2
♣ 8 2

The hand shown is low in offensive strength for a 3♠ pre-empt. Not vulnerable, it is sensible to stretch and bid 3♠, but if vulnerable, it would be circumspect to tone down and open a weak 2♠.

The error some players make is to open 2♠ and then back in with 3♠ later. That course of action is fraught with all the danger of bidding 3♠, without the pre-emptive benefit of bidding it immediately. The tip when opening a weak two or pre-empt is this: bid as high as you dare with weak hands, but having done so, leave the opponents to flounder. The weak two bidder or pre-empter has a duty *not* to bid on unless invited to do so by partner.

Opening in third and fourth seat

In third seat, the point count and shape requirements for a weak two, as for other bids, are a little more flexible. Partner has passed, so if you are not strong, the hand probably belongs to the opponents. At favourable vulnerability, you pick up the following hand and hear two passes to you:

    ♠ K J 9 8 4 3
    ♡ 7 3
    ◇ 9 8
    ♣ 8 5 4

Open 2♠, but only in third seat. Opposite a passed hand it's fair to assume that the opponents, not partner, have the strength and will have to unravel the hand. They can probably make game but your bid might throw them off the trail, get partner off to the right lead, or suggest a sacrifice. In third seat, you might even have a void, or have only five cards in your weak two suit, or perhaps have a 4-card major on the side.

In fourth seat, you would let the deal be thrown in if you were weak so your "weak" two would be about 9-12 HCP, like the following hand:

♠ K 10
♥ A Q J 9 3 2
♦ J 3
♣ 10 9 7

Normally this would be a one-opening but fourth in hand, open 2♥ and hope to buy the contract. You may open a weak 2♠ in fourth seat with a good 8 HCP, taking advantage of holding the "boss" suit, but with anything less, allow the hand to be thrown in.

Responding to a weak two

Since the weak two shows less than opening points, responder needs better than minimum opening points to seek game: about 16+ HCP with no fit, and a sound opening (over 3½ tricks, typically 15+ total points or TP) in a hand with a good fit. With a fit and an even better hand (about 4½ tricks, around 18+ TP), insist on game.

In counting tricks, value the ace, king and even queen of trumps as winners. In the outside suits, count quick tricks (A=1, AK=2, AQ=1½, KQ=1, Kx=½) and shortages (void=2, singleton=1).

Note that weak hands with a fit may still be worth a bid to make life tough for the opponents.

Here is a summary of the main responses:

1.   Pass is the most common reply to a weak two. Pass unless you have either good support for partner, or a terrific hand. Opposite a weak 2♥, what should you do with this hand?

♠ A Q 8 7
♥ 5
♦ K J 6 5 2
♣ K Q 2

Pass. Your side cannot have as much as 26 HCP, and with ill-fitting hands, game is unlikely to make on much less. It is also wrong to try to rescue partner - just pass quickly and hope the opponents come in.

2.   Raising partner's suit (e.g. 2♠:3♠) does not invite game, it
      merely heightens the pre-empt to make it hard for fourth player
      to enter the auction. It is therefore based on weak or moder-
      ate values plus a fit, typically 3-card support:

> ♠ 9 7
> ♡ A J 5
> ◇ A 9 7 2
> ♣ 9 7 5 3

Raise a 2♡ opening to 3♡, attacking the enemy communica-
tions. But if partner opens 2♠, just pass; you have tolerance
for spades but no great enthusiasm for them. It is possible
that 2♠ is the last making contract for either side on this hand.
To heighten a pre-empt, good fit is important, points are not.

3.   Raising partner's suit to game (e.g. 2♠:4♠) may also be a
      pre-empt (usually with four trumps, possibly a shapely hand
      with three trumps), or it may be expecting to make, or some-
      times even a bit of both:

> ♠ K Q 9 7
> ♡ 5
> ◇ K Q 5 2
> ♣ 9 8 6 4

If partner opens 2♠, how should you reply? Bid 4♠. With four
decent trumps and good shape, raise to game irrespective of
strength. Don't try and guess whether you can make game -
just bid it and make the opponents guess instead!

4.   A new suit by responder (e.g. 2♠:3♡) shows a good 5-card
      (probably longer) suit. The change of suit is forcing for one
      round (unless responder is a passed hand), so it should be
      based on better than a bare opening hand, normally 16+ HCP.
      Opener will raise with at least Qx or three small trumps.

> ♠ 4
> ♡ A K J 5 4 2
> ◇ K Q 3
> ♣ A J 7

If partner opens 2♠, bid 3♡ in the hope of finding support.

5.   If interested in game or slam, but wanting to know more about the strength of the weak two, use the 2NT Ogust enquiry.

Ogust

In response to a weak two opening, 2NT should be used not as a natural notrump bid, but to ask how good a hand the weak two bidder has. A popular method using 2NT in this way is called Ogust.

Ogust tells you about your partner's range and suit quality. Use it when you are unsure whether to go to game (or, for that matter, slam) so that you can find out more about partner's hand and decide the appropriate level. After a weak two opening, followed by a 2NT (Ogust) response, opener rebids:

> 3♣ = minimum hand, one top honour (A, K or Q)
> 3♦ = minimum hand, two top honours (AK, AQ or KQ)
> 3♥ = maximum hand, one top honour
> 3♠ = maximum hand, two top honours
> 3NT = solid suit (AKQxxx)

A "minimum" weak two has 6-8 HCP. A "maximum" has 8-10 HCP. Treat 8 HCP as maximum with 6-4 shape or other good features. "Top honours" are the AKQ of the long suit (the weak two suit).

The 2NT bidder finds out about opener's hand and can then sign off in three of the major, bid game or possibly even go to slam.

Partner opens 2♥ and you have this hand:

> ♠ 8 3
> ♥ J 6 2
> ♦ A K 7 2
> ♣ A Q 8 4

Bid 2NT, Ogust. This is a decent opening hand (3-card support plus 15 TP, with over 3½ tricks for partner), so you have prospects for game. If partner replies 3♥, 3♠ or 3NT to your Ogust enquiry, that shows a maximum, and you should push on to 4♥. But if partner shows a minimum (by bidding 3♣ or 3♦), you should bow out in 3♥.

Note that if partner opened a weak 2♠ and you had the hand above, it would be wise to just pass. Opposite a spade bid, this hand is not as good because it has no ruffing value, and a poorer fit. With just 3½ honour tricks and a lacklustre fit, this becomes a very minimum opening hand, and that is not quite enough to look for game opposite a weak two bid.

Sometimes the information Ogust provides about opener's suit quality is most valuable. Knowing that your suit quality is adequate (or not) is of course important when deciding whether to bid slam, and it can also help in deciding whether to bid 3NT. Partner opens 2♥, you respond 2NT Ogust, and partner rebids 3♦, showing minimum points but a good suit. What are your thoughts with this hand:

> ♠ A K 9
> ♥ A 10 7
> ♦ A 9 8
> ♣ J 10 4 2

Bid 3NT, because you can count nine running tricks. You have one top heart honour and partner's Ogust reply promises the other two, so there should be six tricks there, and you have another three outside winners. The opponents might cash the first three club tricks but after that you will be in and happy.

Coping with interference over a weak two opening

If the opponents double a weak two opening, 2NT is still available as Ogust. Ogust is used on invitational hands so an immediate raise of opener's suit, e.g. 2♠:(Dble), 3♠, would be pre-emptive, as usual.

Over the opponents' double, redouble shows a strong hand and invites opener to double anything they run to. Any misfitting 16+ HCP hand would redouble, so a change of suit over the double is no longer forcing; in fact, it would be a rescue, to play.

If the opponents overcall opener's weak 2♥ with a bid of 2♠, then 2NT is still Ogust. Any time 2NT Ogust is available, the raise of partner's suit is purely pre-emptive. However in other overcall auctions, the bidding will be at the 3-level, so Ogust is not available to express forward going values. The raise of opener's suit, e.g. 2♡: (3♣): 3♡, is then mildly invitational, not pre-emptive.

If the opponents overcall opener's weak two, a new suit by responder is still forcing, just as it would have been if the opponents had not bid, e.g. after 2♠: (3♣), now 3♡ is forcing.

Double of an overcall is for penalties, even if you play negative doubles in other situations. Opposite any pre-emptive opening (including a weak two), all doubles by responder are for penalties.

Defending against weak twos

We have seen how to play weak twos, but how should you bid over a weak two by an opponent? The answer is, you should treat it pretty much as if it were a one-opening and all your bids were a level lower.

Double is for takeout, with at least opening points and usually tolerance for all the unbid suits. If you hear a weak 2♠ on your right, what should you do with this hand?

> ♠ 9 2
> ♡ A 8 7 3
> ◇ A Q 8
> ♣ A 4 3 2

Double, for takeout.

Sometimes you will have a choice of calls. An opponent opens 2♠, and you have this hand:

> ♠ 9
> ♡ K 10 7 3
> ◇ K 9 8
> ♣ A K 7 4 2

A takeout double is best. With four cards in the unbid major (and tolerance for all the unbid suits), it is better to double than to overcall 3♣.

An overcall shows a good 5-card suit and around 10-16 HCP, but a 3-level overcall should be slightly stronger or have a longer suit. Your right hand opponent opens 2♥ (weak) and you have this hand:

      ♠ 8 7 6
      ♥ 7 3
      ◇ A J 2
      ♣ A J 10 4 2

Pass. Although shortage in the enemy suit makes action tempting, the hand is not quite good enough for a takeout double or a 3♣ overcall, even if not vulnerable. If the black suits were reversed (that is, you had five spades), then you could try 2♠ - taking advantage of having the "boss" suit, which can outbid them while staying at the same level.

With much stronger hands, make a jump overcall or double and then bid again. Even if you normally play weak jump overcalls, they don't apply over an opponent's pre-empt or weak two: it's more important to be able to show your strong hands. Over a weak 2♠, what call should you make with this hand?

      ♠ A 10
      ♥ K Q J 9 8 3 2
      ◇ A Q 2
      ♣ J

Bid 4♥. This hand is too strong for a simple overcall (especially with this shape), so jump a level. But if your opponent opens 2♠ and you have this hand:

      ♠ 9 7
      ♥ A K Q J 9
      ◇ A 7 2
      ♣ A 8 4

This time it would be wrong to jump to 4♥ - that would be an overstatement of the heart length and playing strength. Instead, start with a takeout double, planning to bid 3♥ over partner's response. Double and then bid again (over a weak response by partner) shows about 17+ points.

A 2NT overcall of a weak two shows a good 15-18 HCP, at *least* one stopper in the enemy suit and a fairly balanced hand (it is never the "Unusual 2NT"). With an even stronger hand, double first and then bid notrumps, or try a direct 3NT. When the opponents open with a weak bid, partner rates to have a few points - and because there is not much space to find out exactly how many, you have to take a few chances. Over a weak 2♠, what should you call with this hand?

    ♠ A K
    ♡ K J 9
    ◊ A J 7 2
    ♣ A 8 4 2

Double, planning to bid 3NT next round.

In passout seat, it is acceptable to act with a hand that is slightly below the normal requirements. If you are a passed hand, you have a degree of further licence in that partner knows any action you take has below opening points. You deal and pass, and hear left hand opponent open 2♡, passed around to you:

    ♠ A J 9 7
    ♡ 2
    ◊ A 8 7 2
    ♣ 10 9 8 4

Double for takeout, especially if you are not vulnerable. You are below normal strength for a takeout double, but other things are in your favour. You may shade the requirements for action when in the passout seat; in fact, partner knows you have done so this time (you are a passed hand). You have spades (which outrank the opposition suit, hearts), and you have the other unbid suits too - an ideal shape.

A cue bid of the enemy suit may be used to invite partner to bid 3NT if holding a stopper in that suit. Of course you must have a very powerful hand to justify making this bid as partner may have nothing. Alternatively, many players use a direct bid of the enemy suit as a Michaels Cue Bid, showing 5-5 or better in the other major and one of the minors. Consider your strategy with the following hand, after an opponent opens a weak 2♠:

    ♠ 9 7
    ♥ A K Q 2
    ♦ A Q 7
    ♣ A K Q J

Start with a takeout double. Raise a 3♥ reply to 4♥. If partner instead replies 3♣ or 3♦, you will bid the enemy suit, 3♠. This does not show anything (except of course a very strong hand), it just forces partner to keep bidding. With spades stopped, partner should then try 3NT.

Weak jump overcalls

Most players who adopt weak two openings play that a jump overcall of the opponent's opening bid is also weak.

    ♠ 9 7
    ♥ K Q 10 7 3 2
    ♦ J 7 2
    ♣ 8 4

You would open this hand with a weak 2♥, and if you play weak jump overcalls, you can make the same bid over an opening one of a minor by the opponents.

However, if the opening bid was 1♠, you would have to bid 3♥ to show the weak jump hand. That is a little excessive on the cards shown, unless you are not vulnerable. Otherwise just pass - it is often wise to have a 7-card suit if your weak jump overcall will take you to the 3-level.

If you play weak jump overcalls, how do you show a hand too strong to make a simple overcall, say 17+ HCP? In fact it is easy: you start with a double, showing 12+ HCP, then you bid again to reveal extra values.

Quiz on weak twos

1. What opening bid would you make with these hands?

(a) ♠ QJ9752 ♡ A3 ♢ 973 ♣ 86	(b) ♠ 8 ♡ 94 ♢ AQ10876 ♣ 9832	(c) ♠ AQ87432 ♡ 43 ♢ 85 ♣ 98
(d) ♠ 52 ♡ KJ8732 ♢ QJ75 ♣ 6	(e) ♠ AK9732 ♡ K43 ♢ 8764 ♣ —	(f) ♠ J98742 ♡ KQ ♢ J75 ♣ 85

2. How would you respond to an opening bid of 2♠ with these hands?

(a) ♠ 97 ♡ 3 ♢ AKQ82 ♣ AQJ43	(b) ♠ J875 ♡ 2 ♢ KQJ43 ♣ 1073	(c) ♠ KQ3 ♡ Q5 ♢ K765 ♣ 9732
(d) ♠ Q5 ♡ AKQ3 ♢ J76 ♣ K982	(e) ♠ 8 ♡ AKQ109 ♢ AKJ8 ♣ AQ2	(f) ♠ 2 ♡ KQJ ♢ QJ82 ♣ AJ872

3. You open 2♡ and partner enquires with 2NT, Ogust. How should you answer with these hands?

(a) ♠ 3 ♡ AQ9864 ♢ 972 ♣ 864	(b) ♠ 975 ♡ AKQ875 ♢ 864 ♣ 8	(c) ♠ 4 ♡ AK10432 ♢ J1086 ♣ 95

Answers to Quiz

1.   (a)   2♠. A routine weak two.

     (b)   Pass, or try 3◇ if not vulnerable. Playing Benjamin Twos,
           only 2♡ and 2♠ are weak, so don't open 2◇!

     (c)   3♠. You're not supposed to bid a weak two with a 7-
           card suit but if you are vulnerable, you might make an
           exception on this hand - minimum, bad texture, bad
           shape.

     (d)   2♡. A 4-card *minor* is no bar to a weak two.

     (e)   1♠. Too good for 2♠ - the void adds to your potential.

     (f)   Pass. Unless you have a very tolerant partner.

2.   (a)   4♠. Go for the major suit game - you have the values
           and you have the fit.

     (b)   4♠. Pre-emptive this time.

     (c)   3♠. Make it harder for them to find their heart fit.

     (d)   2NT, Ogust. If partner is maximum you'll bid game.

     (e)   3♡. If partner supports, head for slam.

     (f)   Pass. Misfitting hands need around 16+ HCP to move.

3.   (a)   3◇. Minimum hand but good suit (i.e. two top honours).

     (b)   3NT. Says your suit has the top three honours, AKQ.

     (c)   3♠. Maximum hand, good suit. With a 6-4 shape, 8
           HCP counts as maximum - especially when the two suits
           are as strong as this.

PLAY HANDS — WEAK TWOS

HAND 1   DLR: North   VUL: Nil

Game raise - setting up a long suit - the A J 10 combination

```
                      ♠ K Q 9 6 5 4
                      ♡ Q J 4
                      ◇ 6 5 3
                      ♣ J
       ♠ 10                          ♠ 8 2
       ♡ A K 5 3 2                   ♡ 10 9 8 7 6
       ◇ Q 7                         ◇ K 8 2
       ♣ Q 9 5 4 3                   ♣ A K 8
                      ♠ A J 7 3
                      ♡ —
                      ◇ A J 10 9 4
                      ♣ 10 7 6 2
```

WEST	NORTH	EAST	SOUTH
	2♠	Pass	4♠
All Pass			

The bidding: With a great spade fit and a void, bid a direct 4♠; even if it doesn't make, it cuts the opponents out of their likely heart game. West's cards are a little flimsy to come in at the 5-level but 4♡ by East-West would have been an easy make.

Lead: ♣A.

The play: Ruff the second club and draw trumps in two rounds. Now set up the long suit, diamonds, while you still have trumps left to control the other suits. In playing an AJ10 combination, plan to finesse twice. Because you are finessing against two honours (K and Q), the first finesse will usually lose, in this case to the ◇Q. However, the next finesse wins unless both missing honours are offside. This time they're not, so 11 tricks can be made.

HAND 2   DLR: East   VUL: NS

Ogust enquiry – ruffing in the short hand

```
                        ♠ K 10 4 3 2
                        ♡ 10
                        ◇ 10 8 4 3
                        ♣ Q 8 5
        ♠ 9 7                          ♠ J 8 6
        ♡ Q 9 2                        ♡ A K J 7 6 5
        ◇ A 9 7 2                      ◇ 6 5
        ♣ A K 7 6                      ♣ J 2
                        ♠ A Q 5
                        ♡ 8 4 3
                        ◇ K Q J
                        ♣ 10 9 4 3
```

WEST	NORTH	EAST	SOUTH
		2♡	Pass
2NT	Pass	3♠	Pass
4♡	All Pass		

The bidding: West's 13 HCP are good ones - a trump honour plus three quick tricks. Add to that the likely ruffing trick from the doubleton, and the hand is worth a try for game. Bid 2NT, Ogust. Partner's 3♠ shows a maximum and a good suit, so try 4♡.

Lead: ◇K, top of a sequence. A trump lead is also reasonable.

The play: It is normal to postpone drawing trumps when a ruff needs to be taken in dummy. If dummy had longer trumps, there would be no urgency to get the ruff but as the cards lie, spades must be played immediately. Even one round of trumps first will allow a good South defender to draw the other two rounds and prevent dummy ruffing the third round of spades. Best play makes ten tricks.

HAND 3   DLR: South VUL: EW

Ogust in a slam auction - guarding against a bad break

```
                    ♠ K 9 4
                    ♡ A K Q J 9
                    ◇ A 5 4 2
                    ♣ 10
        ♠ J 7 6 5              ♠ —
        ♡ 8 6                  ♡ 7 4 2
        ◇ K Q                  ◇ J 9 8 7
        ♣ A 9 7 5 4            ♣ K Q 8 6 3 2
                    ♠ A Q 10 8 3 2
                    ♡ 10 5 3
                    ◇ 10 6 3
                    ♣ J
```

WEST	NORTH	EAST	SOUTH
			2♠
Pass	2NT	Pass	3◇
Pass	6♠	All Pass	

The bidding: Opposite South's weak 2♠, North can conceive of bigger things. South's 3◇ response to Ogust shows a minimum but a good suit – two of the top three spade honours, therefore obviously ♠AQ since North holds the ♠K. North can now count 12 likely tricks - six spades, a diamond and five hearts.

Lead: ◇K.

The play: It looks as if the tricks are there for the taking but could anything go wrong? Only a 4-0 trump break, and even that can be guarded against. Cash ♠Q (or ♠A) first. If both opponents follow, there is no problem. This time, East shows out, marking West with all the missing spades. Lead a low spade from hand, and after West plays low, insert the ♠9, taking the "marked" finesse against West's ♠J. After cashing ♠K, lead ♡9 and overtake with ♡10 to get back to hand in order to draw the last trump.

HAND 4   DLR: West   VUL: Both

Staying low on a misfit – trumping in the short hand

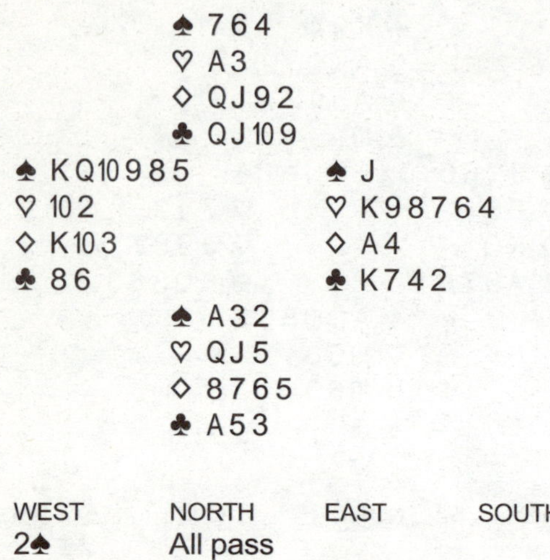

<pre>
                        ♠ 7 6 4
                        ♡ A 3
                        ◇ Q J 9 2
                        ♣ Q J 10 9
      ♠ K Q 10 9 8 5   ♠ J
      ♡ 10 2   ♡ K 9 8 7 6 4
      ◇ K 10 3   ◇ A 4
      ♣ 8 6   ♣ K 7 4 2
                        ♠ A 3 2
                        ♡ Q J 5
                        ◇ 8 7 6 5
                        ♣ A 5 3
</pre>

WEST	NORTH	EAST	SOUTH
2♠	All pass		

The bidding: West, despite having the weakest hand, is the only one able to make a bid. The East collection is uninspiring opposite a partner who has shown a weak spade hand.

Lead: ♣Q.

The play: The usual line in a suit contract is to draw trumps unless you need to first trump in the short hand (the hand with fewer trumps, usually dummy). Here, dummy has only one trump but it can be put to good use if declarer plays ace of diamonds, king of diamonds, trump a diamond. The defenders might foresee this possibility and play a round of trumps to stop the ruff. That stops the overtrick, but the contract still comes home on the heart finesse (low to the king).

STRONG TWO DIAMONDS

The strongest opening bid

Chapter 2

THE BENJAMIN 2◇ OPENING

2◇ is the strongest opening bid in the Benjamin system. It is artificial; the real suit (or notrumps) is shown on the next round. The 2◇ opening is game forcing unless opener rebids 2NT, and even then responder will bid on except with a complete bust.

Open 2◇ with all hands of 23+ HCP, and most unbalanced hands of 22 HCP. You may open a hand with somewhat less in high card strength so long as it contains ten playing tricks.

Playing tricks

Unbalanced hands with powerful suits have a trick-taking potential greater than the high card strength would indicate. This potential is valued as playing tricks. Playing tricks reflect the number of tricks you would expect to make with your long suit as trumps — offensive tricks, rather than defensive tricks which are those you would expect to make if the opponents play the hand. In calculating playing tricks, assume every card after the first three in your long suits will be a trick:

   ♠ A Q J 8 7 6 4
   ♡ A K Q
   ◇ A 6
   ♣ 5

This hand values at ten playing tricks: at least six tricks in spades (it is likely a trick will be lost to ♣K, but then assume every spade after the first three will be a winner), three tricks in hearts, and a trick in diamonds. Open 2◇.

   ♠ K Q J
   ♡ J
   ◇ K Q J 7 6 4
   ♣ A Q 2

This hand comes in around 8½ playing tricks. The diamonds are worth five, and the spades two tricks. The clubs may produce one or two tricks; count this as 1½ tricks. The hand is not strong enough to open 2◇, but is an ideal 2♣ opening as we shall see in the next chapter.

      ♠ A K Q 9 7
      ♡ 5
      ◇ A K Q 9 2
      ♣ A K

This hand has 12 playing tricks! Although they are by no means certain tricks, slam should be a good chance even opposite a yarborough, so long as partner has a fit for one of your suits. Open 2◇ with hopes of big things to come.

Unbalanced 2◇ openings

All hands of 23+ HCP are opened with a bid of 2◇ but fewer HCP are OK if the hand contains about ten playing tricks. For example:

      ♠ A K Q 9 4
      ♡ A
      ◇ A K Q 9
      ♣ 9 7 2

This hand is good enough to game force. You have five playing tricks in spades, one in hearts, and hopefully four in diamonds. Most unbalanced hands of 22 HCP are strong enough to open 2◇.

If the hand meets the ten trick requirement it could have as few as 16 HCP:

      ♠ A K 9 8 7 2
      ♡ A K Q 7 2
      ◇ 8
      ♣ 2

A loser in each minor and a likely loser in spades still leaves this a ten trick hand. Open 2◇ then show your spades. If they fail to excite partner, try hearts instead.

However:

♠ J
♡ 9 8
♢ A K Q J 10 8 7 6 5 2
♣ —

This hand is worth ten tricks but don't open 2♢. Partner will expect more high card strength and may misjudge the hand. Open 5♢, a blunt pre-empt, or a more exploratory 1♢.

The Benjamin 2♢ opening is completely artificial; it says nothing about diamonds. The real suit is shown on the next round and promises five. The normal rules of shape-showing apply: first bid the longest suit, or the higher-ranking of two 5-card (or two 6-card) suits. With this hand:

♠ A J 8 4 2
♡ A K Q 7 6
♢ Q
♣ A K

Open 2♢ to show the huge hand, then bid spades, the higher-ranked of the two 5-card suits.

If your longest suit was only four cards, you would have a balanced hand and would rebid notrumps. The only exception is the 4-4-4-1 hand:

♠ A K Q 3
♡ 7
♢ A K 9 2
♣ A K J 5

You open 2♢. Say partner replies 2♡, which is the negative response and completely artificial (see next section). What now?

Normally an unbalanced hand has a 5-card suit which you can show, but the 4-4-4-1 shape is the rare exception. If the singleton was the ace or king a notrump rebid could be condoned, but on the hand as it stands, it is best to bid 2♠, the cheapest 4-card suit.

Responding to the Benjamin 2◇

The negative response to the Benjamin 2◇ is 2♡, and shows any hand of 0-7 HCP.

> ♠ Q 9 8 6 4
> ♡ 8 6
> ◇ 9 7 5
> ♣ 5 3 2

Over partner's 2◇ opening, you would bid 2♡, the negative response, to put the brakes on any slam aspirations partner may harbour. You are still committed to game however, and will reveal the 5-card spade suit on the next round. Introducing a suit as your first natural call in any Benjamin auction indicates at least five cards; otherwise, strive to bid notrumps or raise partner's suit.

As in other game-forcing auctions, the principle of fast arrival applies - jump raising to game shows no extras - so just raise partner's suit one level if you are interested in more. If partner opens 2◇ and you respond 2♡ (negative) with the hand below, what should you do next if partner rebids 2♠:

> ♠ J 6 4
> ♡ J 8 6
> ◇ A 9 7 5
> ♣ 5 3 2

Partner should have 5+ spades so you intend to raise, but how high? Your side is committed to game, which is precisely why there is no rush for you to bid it. Raise to 3♠, leaving room for partner to initiate a slam investigation if desired. In light of your initial negative response, partner should not expect you to have more.

In answer to the Benjamin 2◇ opening, any response other than 2♡ is a positive, promising 8+ HCP. Bidding a suit promises five cards, whereas 2NT is the balanced positive. A positive response to a Benjamin 2◇ indicates slam is likely.

If partner opens 2◇, how should you respond with the following hand:

♠ K Q 8 7 5
♥ K 5 3
♦ 9 7 6
♣ 9 2

Although the hand is balanced, it is best to respond 2♠, showing 5+ spades and 8+ HCP. If partner bids a red suit next you can show a fit by raising, whereas if partner bids 2NT you will raise to 3NT, or if partner bids 3♣ you might also try 3NT for lack of alternatives. You have already shown your 8 HCP so it is up to partner to look for slam if appropriate.

What is the response to a 2♦ opening with the hand below:

♠ 8 6
♥ K Q 10 4 3
♦ Q 10 9 7
♣ K 9

Since the negative response to a Benjamin 2♦ opening is 2♥, bid 3♥ to show a positive with hearts. But if you have no 5-card suit:

♠ Q 10 6 2
♥ K 9 3
♦ Q 9 7
♣ K 10 8

With this hand, respond to partner's 2♦ opening with a call of 2NT, the balanced positive response. Stayman applies when notrumps is the first natural bid of the auction, so opener may bid 3♣ to ask for a major. Other suit bids by opener are natural and promise 5+ cards. Even if you play transfers, they do not apply over a notrump bid by responder - it would be wrong to make the strong 2♣ or 2♦ opener transfer, because then the weak hand would declare more often.

We have seen that the positive responses to a Benjamin 2♦ opening are to bid a 5-card suit, or to bid 2NT if balanced. As we know, the only hand shape that fits into neither category is the 4-4-4-1.

With such a hand, you may bid the cheapest of your suits, even though that promises a 5-carder. An alternative is to make the "negative" response of 2♡, and then try to "catch up" later.

Showing strong balanced hands

The old Goren method was 2NT=22-24, 3NT=25-27 HCP. Under that approach, you could open one of a suit with a balanced 21-count and be stuck there, even if partner had 5 HCP, enough for game. Also, the 22-24 range was too wide.

There is a better way. Playing Benjamin Twos, we have seen that all hands of 23+ HCP open 2◊. Unbalanced hands then rebid a long suit. Logically enough, balanced hands of 23+ HCP open 2◊ then rebid in notrumps. Below is an outline of how we show strong balanced hands:

19-20 points, balanced: Open one of a suit, jump in notrumps

21-22 points, balanced: Open 2NT

(Variation: Some experienced partnerships use a 2NT opening to show about 6-11 HCP and 5-5 in the minors – the sort of hand that would have qualified for the "Unusual 2NT" overcall if the opponents had opened. If you adopt this approach, use the 2♣ opening followed by a 2NT rebid to show the balanced 21-22 point hand. This book doesn't use this treatment.)

23-24 points, balanced: Open 2◊, rebid 2NT

25-28 points, balanced: Open 2◊, rebid 3NT

29-30 points, balanced: Open 2◊, rebid 4NT

31-32 points, balanced: Open 2◊, rebid 5NT

The Benjamin 2◊ auctions above all assume partner makes a negative 2♡ response. Over a positive response by partner, there are no set rebids but the 2◊ opener would not allow the bidding to die in game if holding 25+ points.

    ♠ K 10
    ♡ A Q 8
    ◇ K Q 9 8
    ♣ A K 8 7

This is a good hand for a 2NT opening in modern standard. The fact that you have all suits covered is an added bonus, it's not essential.

Although notrump openings are based on high card points, you may sometimes upgrade a hand by a point because of other features including a good 5-card suit:

    ♠ K 2
    ♡ A 10 9
    ◇ Q J 10
    ♣ A K Q J 10

It would be conservative to open this 20 HCP hand at the 1-level. The perfect 5-card suit, excellent intermediates and lack of any negative features make this hand worth an extra point. Open 2NT. With a stronger hand like the one below:

    ♠ A 7
    ♡ A Q 8
    ◇ K 9 8
    ♣ A K Q J 8

Open 2◇, showing 23+ points. Partner will probably reply 2♡, the negative response, after which you should bid 2NT, showing a balanced hand of precisely 23-24 points. If that 5-card suit was a major, however, you might choose to show it rather than bid notrumps immediately.

If notrumps is the first natural bid of the auction, for example a 2NT opening or a 2◇ : 2♡, 2NT rebid, then responder may use Stayman. If you play transfer bids in response to a 1NT or 2NT opening, then you should play them over the 2NT (or 3NT) rebid by opener, thereby allowing the strong hand to declare. But remember, Stayman and transfers never apply if your side has already bid a genuine suit.

After a 2◇ opening, the only time either player may pass below game is after the bidding has commenced 2◇ : 2♡ (negative), 2NT. Even then, responder will push on with just two points:

      ♠ Q987
      ♡ 86
      ◇ 98753
      ♣ 53

Partner opened 2◇, so you responded 2♡, the negative. What should you do if partner now rebids 2NT, showing a balanced hand of 23-24 points? Your meagre collection is enough to go for game, so search for a major suit fit: bid 3♣, Stayman.

A notrump call limits that hand, leaving partner in a good position to assess slam prospects. With the hand below, partner opened 2◇, you responded 2♡ negative, and partner rebid 3NT, showing 25-28 points, balanced. What now?

      ♠ AJ
      ♡ J98
      ◇ 10982
      ♣ 10987

Bid 4NT, inviting slam. Opener's 3NT was the first natural bid of the auction, so we know that normal principles apply as they would in response to an opening notrump bid - so raising to 4NT is not Blackwood, it just asks partner to bid slam with a maximum.

The Gambling 3NT

With all hands of 23+ HCP, we open 2◇. What, then, would an opening bid of 3NT show? The answer may be surprising: an opening bid of 3NT shows a solid 7-card or 8-card minor with little or no strength outside:

      ♠ 7
      ♡ 86
      ◇ AKQ10853
      ♣ J53

Open 3NT. If partner has a couple of tricks for you, you might make 3NT. Then again, the opponents might massacre you with the right lead. No wonder it is called the "gambling 3NT", but don't be put off by the name: although you will often go down, you may still show a profit if you've talked the opponents out of a game.

Of course, if 3NT looks disastrous, responder doesn't have to pass. To play in opener's suit, just bid clubs – 4♣, 5♣, 6♣ or 7♣ according to strength - and opener will "correct" the contract to diamonds if that is the long suit. If opener's long suit is clubs, opener just passes – the responder is in charge of deciding the level.

Opposite a gambling 3NT, a bid of four of a major by responder would be based on a self-sufficient 6-card or longer suit.

Coping with interference over the 2◊ opening

If the opponents double or bid over the 2◊ opening, responder is not obliged to answer the 2◊ bid, as would otherwise be the case. The opposition interference has ensured that partner will get another chance to bid, so just pass to show the negative response.

Any bid would show a positive, and double (or redouble) would be for penalties. Some players amend this structure by playing double for takeout if the opponents interfere over a 2◊ opening, but this is only by agreement with partner.

Showing strong hands after the opponents open

If the opponents have already opened the bidding (e.g. 1♡) and you then bid 2◊, that would not be the Benjamin 2◊ – it is just a normal overcall. So how can you show a superstrong hand in such a situation?

The old approach was to bid the opponents' suit (also known as a "cue bid of the enemy suit") which has long been a standard method to force partner to keep bidding to game. The modern alternative is to double first (for takeout) and then bid the enemy suit next round. (If you play Michaels Cue Bids, you will need to follow this latter approach.)

Quiz on Benjamin 2◇

1.   What opening bid would you make with these hands?

   (a) ♠ A K J 8   (b) ♠ 4   (c) ♠ A K Q
        ♡ K Q 3 2   ♡ A K Q J 8 4 3   ♡ A Q J
        ◇ —   ◇ A K Q   ◇ Q J 9 7 2
        ♣ A K Q J 9   ♣ 8 7   ♣ Q 3

2.   Your partner opens 2◇. What response should you make?

   (a) ♠ 8 7 6   (b) ♠ A 7 5   (c) ♠ J 9 4 2
        ♡ 4 3 2   ♡ K Q 9 7 5 2   ♡ K 9 7
        ◇ 9 7 5 3   ◇ 9 7   ◇ Q 10 7 5
        ♣ 7 5 2   ♣ 10 7   ♣ K 10

3.   You opened 2◇ and partner bid 2♡. What should you now call?

   (a) ♠ A 4 2   (b) ♠ K Q 5   (c) ♠ A J 10 4 2
        ♡ A K Q 2   ♡ A Q   ♡ K 7
        ◇ A   ◇ K Q J 9 7   ◇ A K Q J 9
        ♣ A K 9 8 6   ♣ A Q 5   ♣ A

4.   You opened 2◇ and partner bid 2♠. What next?

   (a) ♠ A K 2   (b) ♠ Q   (c) ♠ 9 7
        ♡ A K 3 2   ♡ A K Q 9   ♡ A K 8 5
        ◇ 5 2   ◇ A K J 7 4 2   ◇ A K Q 3
        ♣ A K Q 6   ♣ A K   ♣ A K 3

Answers to Quiz

1   (a)   2◇, showing any hand of 23+ points.

        (b)   2◇. With ten playing tricks, even 19 HCP is plenty.

        (c)   2NT, showing a balanced 21-22 count.

2.   (a)   2♡, the negative response, showing 0-7 HCP.

        (b)   3♡, natural and positive. 2♡ would be the negative.

        (c)   2NT, the balanced positive.

3.   (a)   3♣. Don't raise hearts – remember, partner's 2♡ was
               just negative.

        (b)   2NT. Showing 23-24 points and a balanced hand.

        (c)   2♠. With two 5-card suits, bid the higher-ranked first.

4.   (a)   3♠. Partner should have five spades, so you have a fit.

        (b)   3◇. Good hands, like good wines, should often be al-
               lowed to mature slowly.

        (c)   2NT. And await developments.

PLAY HANDS — THE BENJAMIN 2◊

HAND 5   DLR: North   VUL: NS

The 2NT rebid - gaining entries by overtaking

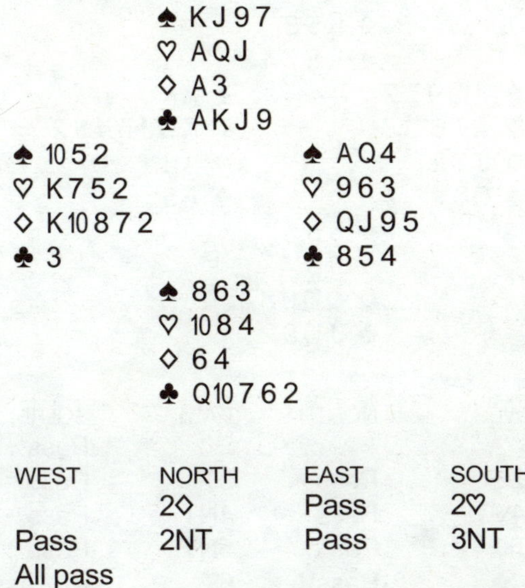

<table>
<tr><td></td><td>♠ K J 9 7
♡ A Q J
◊ A 3
♣ A K J 9</td><td></td></tr>
<tr><td>♠ 10 5 2
♡ K 7 5 2
◊ K 10 8 7 2
♣ 3</td><td></td><td>♠ A Q 4
♡ 9 6 3
◊ Q J 9 5
♣ 8 5 4</td></tr>
<tr><td></td><td>♠ 8 6 3
♡ 10 8 4
◊ 6 4
♣ Q 10 7 6 2</td><td></td></tr>
</table>

WEST	NORTH	EAST	SOUTH
	2◊	Pass	2♡
Pass	2NT	Pass	3NT
All pass			

The bidding: North's 2NT rebid shows a balanced 23-24 points. It's not forcing, but South has enough to shoot for game.

Lead: ◊Q.

The play: Declarer can count five club tricks plus the two red aces; that's two short of the required total. After the defenders knock out the ◊A, it will be fatal to lose the lead. However, if the heart finesse is working, two extra tricks can be made there.

To finesse twice in hearts, declarer needs to get to dummy twice. Cash ♣AK (unblocking) then overtake ♣J with ♣Q in order to get to dummy to lead hearts for the first finesse. It works! Now lead the ♣9 and overtake with the ♣10 to get to dummy again. Cash the last club then repeat the heart finesse. Making nine tricks.

HAND 6   DLR: East   VUL: EW

Slam after a positive - utilising entries for a ruffing finesse

```
                          ♠ Q 5 4 3
                          ♡ 10
                          ◇ K 5 3
                          ♣ K 8 7 4 3
        ♠ J 10 9 7 2                      ♠ A K
        ♡ A 7 6                           ♡ K Q J 5 4 3 2
        ◇ J 7 2                           ◇ A 6
        ♣ Q 6                             ♣ A 5
                          ♠ 8 6
                          ♡ 9 8
                          ◇ Q 10 9 8 4
                          ♣ J 10 9 2
```

WEST	NORTH	EAST	SOUTH
		2◇	Pass
2♠	Pass	3♡	Pass
4♡	Pass	4NT	Pass
5◇	Pass	5NT	Pass
6♣	Pass	6♡	All pass

The bidding: East has ten tricks, enough for 2◇. After West shows a positive plus heart support, slam is likely. Blackwood reveals both minor suit kings are missing, so East stops in small slam.

Lead: ♣J, covered by the ♣Q, ♣K and ♣A.

The play: Declarer has a loser in each minor, so spades must be set up to provide discards. Dummy's only entries are in trumps, so after winning the first trick and cashing the ♡K, declarer must unblock the ♠AK before leading a low trump to dummy's ♡A.

Now lead the ♠J. If North follows with a low spade, declarer should discard the losing diamond. This type of play is known as a "ruffing finesse". If the queen is with North, it is trapped and will be ruffed; if it is with South, the finesse loses, but the minor suit losers get discarded on the spades. With the finesse working, declarer can make all 13 tricks, using the ♡7 as an entry back to dummy.

HAND 7   DLR: South   VUL: Both

Finding fit before bidding slam - ruffing a winner to create an entry

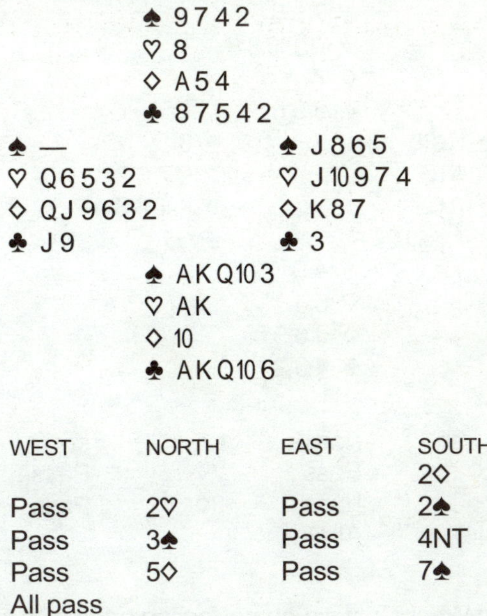

WEST	NORTH	EAST	SOUTH
			2◊
Pass	2♡	Pass	2♠
Pass	3♠	Pass	4NT
Pass	5◊	Pass	7♠
All pass			

The bidding: South has 12 likely tricks if a fit is found. The auction is game-forcing so the raise to 3♠ is actually stronger than a jump to 4♠. When North shows an ace, 7♠ must be a good bet.

Lead: ◊Q.

The play: After winning ◊A, declarer draws a round or two of trumps, and observes the bad break. East is known to hold all the missing trumps, so the finesse against the ♠J is "marked", known to be working. However, with the ◊A already gone, how can declarer get to dummy? Play ♡AK, ruffing the second round. For once it's not a mistake to trump a winner! Now lead spades for the marked finesse: if East plays low, insert the ♠10, knowing it will win.

HAND 8   DLR: West   VUL: Nil

Finding 3NT - preserving an entry and overtaking to set up a suit

```
                    ♠ 7 6 5
                    ♡ Q J 10 8 6
                    ◇ 7
                    ♣ J 9 8 6
        ♠ K J 9 4 3              ♠ 8
        ♡ A K                    ♡ 9 7 3 2
        ◇ A Q                    ◇ K 10 9 8 4 2
        ♣ A K 10 5               ♣ Q 7
                    ♠ A Q 10 2
                    ♡ 5 4
                    ◇ J 6 5 3
                    ♣ 4 3 2
```

WEST	NORTH	EAST	SOUTH
2◇	Pass	2♡	Pass
2♠	Pass	3◇	Pass
3NT	All Pass		

The bidding: West shows a game-forcing hand with spades. After East calls 3◇, 3NT must be bid while there's still a chance.

Lead: ♡Q.

The play: After winning the heart lead, declarer goes to cash ◇A then ◇Q. When North shows out, it is known that the diamonds won't run. Therefore declarer needs an entry to get to dummy to force out the ◇J, as well as the entry back to enjoy those diamonds. The ♣Q will be there as an entry later, but firstly the ◇K must be utilised as an entry: *overtake* the ◇Q with the king so you can continue playing diamonds to get rid of that knavish ◇J.

STRONG TWO CLUBS

At least eight playing tricks

Chapter 3
THE BENJAMIN 2♣ OPENING

The Benjamin 2♣ is the most distinctive of the Benjamin openings and is sometimes misunderstood and misapplied. It was invented to show the traditional Acol Two bid – a hand with a strong suit but not quite strong enough to insist on game, therefore not quite strong enough to open 2◇ in the Benjamin method. 2♣ is artificial so the real suit is shown on the next round.

Requirements

The Benjamin 2♣ opening shows a hand with a long suit and a good eight or nine playing tricks. A common misconception is that all 19-21 HCP hands should open 2♣. Wrong! However, a good guideline is that hands of 19-21 HCP *with a 6-card suit* are suitable:

    ♠ A Q 10
    ♡ K 9 4
    ◇ A K Q J 9 7
    ♣ 9

This hand is ideal for a Benjamin 2♣: it is worth over eight playing tricks and it has a good 6-card suit. If you were not playing Benjamin Twos, you would open this hand 1◇ leading to two possible problems. Firstly, you could be left there when partner has a few points, and miss a game. Secondly, if partner does respond, say 1♡ or 1♠, the hand is too good for a non-forcing 3◇ rebid, yet nor does any other bid describe the hand accurately.

You may open 2♣ with as few as 16 HCP if your hand has over eight playing tricks:

♠ A 5 4
♡ 9
♢ A K Q 10 9 7 2
♣ K 2

Another perfect Benjamin 2♣ and, once again, a hand that it would be hard to do justice to otherwise. But with minimal honour strength, don't open 2♣ with a bare eight tricks:

♠ A K Q
♡ 9 3
♢ K Q J 9 7 2
♣ J 7

With this hand, 1♢ is plenty. Sure, your hand is worth a likely eight playing tricks but with only 16 HCP you shouldn't be stretching the trick requirement as well. Your jump to 3♢ on the next round will show your hand nicely and if game is a good prospect, you should reach it.

Nor should you open 2♣ when your hand has plenty of tricks but too few points:

♠ A K Q J 9 8 7 6
♡ 5
♢ Q 7 5
♣ J

Open this hand 4♠ or 1♠ according to taste. Minimum strength for a 2♣ opening is 16 HCP, or a point or two less with decent defensive potential (such as a couple of aces).

You may have heard it said that any hand of 19-21 HCP should open 2♣, but expert style is to open ordinary 19 or 20 HCP hands which lack a 6-card suit with a bid of one:

♠ K 5 4
♡ J 2
♢ A K Q J 9
♣ K Q 2

Open this hand 1◇, planning to jump in notrumps on the next round. If partner lacks the six points needed to respond to your opening 1-bid, you won't have missed a game, and if partner does have six points and responds, the jump rebid in notrumps describes your hand effectively.

      ♠ K 5 4
      ♡ J
      ◇ A K Q J 9
      ♣ K Q 7 2

With this hand you should open 1◇, not a Benjamin 2♣. Partner will respond to a one-opening with six points, and you plan to then jump-shift to 3♣ with this hand. A jump-shift by opener shows about 19+ points and is game forcing (unlike jumping in the opened suit which shows 16-18 points), a good description of a hand like this.

We have seen that hands of about 19-20 HCP with a 5-card suit can generally be well described by opening one of a suit then jump-shifting (if unbalanced) or jumping in notrumps (if balanced). With just a 5-card suit, it is only necessary to open a Benjamin 2♣ with maximum points, normally 21-22 HCP:

      ♠ A K Q J 2
      ♡ 7 6
      ◇ A K 2
      ♣ A 3 2

Open 2♣ and rebid your powerful 5-card major. However if the 5-card suit were a minor, best would be to open the hand 2NT, despite the heart weakness. We are not so desperate to show minors and besides, if you start with 2♣ and then show a minor you will be at the 3-level, where you would prefer to have a 6-card suit backing you up.

Any hand of 23+ HCP is strong enough to open 2◇; even 22 HCP and a 6-card suit will almost always be too good for 2♣. If you open a Benjamin 2♣, your rebid is not forcing - partner with a worthless or near worthless hand may leave you in the suit. If you have two suits and are keen to show both, prefer to open 2◇ in a borderline situation:

> ♠ A K 9 7 5
> ♡ A K Q J 2
> ◇ K 3
> ♣ 3

It would be dangerous to open this hand 2♣, because whichever suit you rebid might be hopeless for partner, who would pass when game might be a make in the other suit. For example, a partner holding this hand:

> ♠ 4
> ♡ 9 8 7 5 4
> ◇ 8 7 6
> ♣ 8 7 6 5

would pass if the bidding went 2♣: 2◇, 2♠, and the easy heart game would be missed. Prefer to stretch a point or two and open 2◇, game forcing, so at least you know you will have a chance to show both your suits. However:

> ♠ A K 8 7 6 2
> ♡ K
> ◇ A K 3 2
> ♣ Q J

Here you would happily open 2♣. Your spade rebid gives partner the important information about the hand; you'll shed no tears if you never get the chance to show that minor suit.

In summary, then, a 2♣ opening will have:

- a 6-card or longer suit and about 19-21 HCP (a little less with the requisite playing strength of a *good* 8-9 tricks) *or*
- a strong 5-card suit (normally a major) and about 21-22 HCP.

Responding to 2♣ with weak hands

The negative response is the next suit up, 2◊, which is made on any hand of 0-7 HCP.

    ♠ A J 9 7 5 2
    ♡ 4 2
    ◊ 8 6
    ♣ 9 7 4

If partner opens 2♣, you should respond 2◊ with this hand, showing 0-7 HCP. It is true that you have a useful collection and indeed, you will bid your spades next round and press on to game. Your negative response doesn't cause the bidding to die: you will always bid on with 5-7 HCP and will strive to with less.

Even if you respond 2◊, negative, a new suit by you later is forcing for one round:

    ♠ Q J 9 7 5 2
    ♡ 5
    ◊ J 6 2
    ♣ 9 7 4

Over opener's 2♡ rebid you can venture 2♠, taking comfort in the thought that you have shown a negative already. If partner supports spades there should be a game there but if partner persists with hearts, you'll give up.

Whereas a new suit by responder is forcing, even after a negative, bidding 2NT or raising partner's suit is only invitational. After the bidding goes 2♣: 2◊ (by you), 2♡, what do you do with this hand:

    ♠ 2
    ♡ Q 8 5
    ◊ J 10 9 8 5 2
    ♣ 9 6 4

The queen in partner's suit generally adds a trick and a singleton outside the trump suit usually adds at least a trick to the potential of the hand too. With two tricks to add to partner's eight or more, you are too good for an invitational 3♡. Bid 4♡, taking a little pressure off partner in the bidding and adding a little in the play!

Partner opens 2♣, you respond 2◇ with the hand below, and partner rebids 2♠. What should you do next?

> ♠ K 5
> ♡ 5 3
> ◇ J 9 4 3
> ♣ 10 9 8 6 2

Raise to 3♠. Partner will have six spades or a good 5-carder. Notrumps is unappealing with the heart weakness.

Responding to 2♣ with strong hands

In response to a Benjamin 2♣, any bid other than 2◇ is a positive, promising 8+ HCP. Suit bids promise five cards while 2NT is the balanced positive. Of course, any positive response is forcing to game.

What reply to a 2♣ opening would you make with this hand:

> ♠ 2
> ♡ K 8 7 6 4
> ◇ K Q 9 4 2
> ♣ 7 5

Bid 2♡, the higher-ranked of two 5-card suits.

Again, partner opens 2♣. You have this hand:

> ♠ Q 10 8 5
> ♡ K 10 3
> ◇ Q 10 3
> ♣ K 9 5

Bid 2NT, showing a balanced hand of 8+ HCP. After that, the most straightforward approach is to return to the general principle that since 2NT is the first natural bid, 3♣ is Stayman. (If you wish to break from this general principle and play 3♣ here as natural instead of Stayman, you must be clear on that with partner.)

Although the negative response to a 2♣ (or 2◇) opening implies 0-7 HCP, the modern style is that it may also be made on better hands, as a "waiting" bid to find out what opener has. Think about your response to a 2♣ opening with this hand:

> ♠ K J 9 7
> ♡ A 10 7 4
> ◇ 4
> ♣ Q 10 6 2

The 4-4-4-1 shape is awkward, because bidding a suit should show a 5-carder. Consider expanding your use of the "negative" response of 2◇ to include hands like this which have nothing useful to call. If you respond 2◇ with the hand above, you can then try 3NT over partner's expected 3◇ rebid, or look for slam if partner bids one of the other suits.

Even though partner will expect you to have 0-7 HCP, it is quite safe to start with a 2◇ response on stronger hands too since partner will never leave you there. Also, because the 2♣ opener's rebid is well-defined, responder is well-placed to steer the contract.

> ♠ A 9 7
> ♡ 4
> ◇ J 9 8 7 4
> ♣ K J 6 2

With this hand, the positive response to a Benjamin 2♣ would be 3◇, which cramps the auction (for example, it becomes awkward for partner to show clubs) and is unappealing with such a poor suit. Better may be 2◇, "negative or waiting". You can still force to game from there and if partner's long suit is a minor, you can investigate slam.

Use of the "negative" response as a waiting manoeuvre may also be considered when answering a Benjamin 2◊ opening, but is more dangerous because opener's upper strength is not known. The 2◊ opener may have 25 points, in which case a positive response makes slam clear whereas the false negative keeps opener in the dark.

Bidding after a negative response

Opener shows the real suit on the first rebid. A bid of 2♡ or 2♠ could be just a 5-card suit; 3♣ or 3◊ will almost always be at least six cards in length. Most commonly, opener will choose one of these rebids:

- 2♡/♠ = 5+ card suit (usually 6+ cards)
- 3♣/◊ = 6+ card suit (almost certainly)

Although rare, other rebids by opener are possible:

- 2NT = eight tricks or a bit more, with a long minor but suitable for notrumps
- 3♡/♠ = nine tricks with a strong suit (usually 7+ cards)
- 3NT = nine tricks with a long minor, suitable for notrumps
- 4-suit = long, strong suit & 9½ tricks (4♣/◊ can be ten tricks, but did not open 2◊ as unwilling to force to game in a minor)

Most of the time you will just bid your suit at the lowest level; don't feel the need to do anything fancy:

       ♠ A K 7 6 5 2
       ♡ A K 4
       ◊ 9
       ♣ A K 5

You open 2♣ and partner responds 2◊, negative. You have a likely nine tricks but with such an empty spade suit you'll be embarrassed if you get a bad spade break and a bust for dummy so exercise restraint with a gentle 2♠ rebid. This also allows partner to introduce hearts at a comfortable level if desired. You have already shown a big hand by opening 2♣ so partner will strive to respond.

Although it was originally envisaged that a 2♣ opening followed by notrumps would be big and balanced, this book follows the alternative treatment whereby all 23+ balanced hands open 2◇, freeing up the 2♣ opening followed by a notrump rebid to show a long minor hand. After opening 2♣ and hearing the 2◇ negative response, what should opener rebid with this hand:

    ♠ Q 9
    ♡ K 9
    ◇ A K Q 10 9 8 7 5
    ♣ A

Assuming the diamonds run, you have nine tricks once you get the lead. Try 3NT, a gamble that will usually pay off.

Bidding after a positive response

All bids are now forcing to game, so there is no need to jump:

    ♠ A K Q J 9
    ♡ K 10
    ◇ A 9 5
    ♣ A J 3

You open 2♣ and partner responds 2♡, positive with five hearts. The positive response commits your side at least to game, but it's not a race: bid 2♠, and explore from there. If partner raises, you will be happy to play game or slam in spades. If partner repeats hearts, you'll support. Or if partner calls 3♣ or 3◇, try 3NT.

It is often best for opener *not* to show a fit for responder's suit immediately. With the following hand, you open 2♣ and hear responder bid 3♣, a positive with five clubs. What should you do?

    ♠ QJ
    ♡ AKJ943
    ◇ AQ
    ♣ QJ9

Bid 3♡. There is no rush to show the club fit. Bidding hearts may help you to a better spot, or may just help partner judge how well the hands meld together.

Coping with interference over the 2♣ opening

If an opponent doubles or bids over the 2♣ opening, there is no need to respond diamonds as a negative: just pass, and partner will have another chance to bid anyway. A standard approach over interference is that any bid by responder is positive, forcing to game.

If North opens 2♣ and the next player overcalls 2♡, what should South do with this hand:

    ♠ KQ5
    ♡ 1097
    ◇ 987
    ♣ J432

Pass. If partner bids spades on the next round, you will raise to 4♠. If, on the other hand, partner bids a minor, you will then bid the enemy suit, 3♡, to ask partner to bid 3NT with a heart stopper.

If North opens 2♣ and East doubles, what should South bid holding these cards:

    ♠ 85
    ♡ QJ97
    ◇ KQJ43
    ♣ 96

You were planning to bid 3◇ but over the double, a frugal 2◇ is enough. After all, with the negative hand you would pass (the double keeps the bidding open, so there is no compulsion to respond) so even 2◇ is positive in this instance.

Defending against strong bids

We have seen how to show strong hands using the Benjamin 2♣ and 2♦ openings, but now let us look at how to upset the opponents when they make artificial strong openings. You might think pass would be automatic when facing such a strong enemy but a tactical bid by you can often push the opponents around and get partner off to the right lead. Your bid will often go unpunished because the opponents usually want to show their suits rather than take a stab in the dark with a double when they have no idea of each other's distribution.

Double of an artificial bid generally shows that suit, so unless an alternative defence had been discussed, double of a Benjamin 2♣ would show clubs and double of a Benjamin 2♦ would show diamonds. Jump overcalls over their strong openings are always weak.

Some systems such as Precision use a 1♣ opening to show their strong hands, to keep the bidding low for maximum exploration. If you allow yourself to be cowed into silence they will succeed in their aim, but the bidding is so low that you can safely come in on most hands. Disruption should be the aim; to show a good hand, pass first and come in later.

Against a Benjamin 2♣ or 2♦ opener, the bidding is a little higher so there is a bit more danger of being doubled and not so much need to push them up either. But with the right quality suit and at the right vulnerability, still be prepared to stick your neck out. At favourable vulnerability, over a Benjamin 2♣ or 2♦ opening, with the following hand:

      ♠ K Q 10 8 7 6
      ♡ 10
      ♦ 10 9 5
      ♣ 6 4 3

Bid 3♠, a spoiling action that is justified by the vulnerability.

Quiz on Benjamin 2♣

1.	What opening bid would you make with these hands?

	(a)	(b)	(c)
♠	AK2	86	AK86
♡	AKQJ108	AKQ108642	AK
◇	Q64	9	K1097
♣	8	83	Q109

2.	Your partner opens 2♣. What response would you make?

	(a)	(b)	(c)
♠	8	KQ752	Q1094
♡	KQJ97	AKQ4	Q987
◇	972	—	K10
♣	9754	Q732	Q102

3.	You opened 2♣ and heard partner respond 2◇, negative. What next?

	(a)	(b)	(c)
♠	97	K5	AKQJ1086
♡	AKQ	K9	32
◇	AKQJ72	AKQ9864	86
♣	86	K5	AK

4.	The auction commences 2♣ by you, 3♣ by partner. What now?

	(a)	(b)	(c)
♠	KQJ1072	KQJ1072	A6
♡	AKQ	AKQ	2
◇	A72	8	AKQ10992
♣	8	A72	KQ75

Answers to Quiz

1.   (a)   2♣. You have over eight playing tricks. You are also in
              the typical 19-21 HCP range, but you would still bid this
              way with slightly less.

      (b)   4♥. You have an 8-trick hand but with only 9 HCP you're
              not strong enough to open even 1♥, let alone 2♣.

      (c)   1◇. Balanced hands of 19-20 HCP are strong but not
              spectacular. Open one, then jump in notrumps.

2.   (a)   2◇. Not good enough for a positive response. You will
              bid your hearts next round.

      (b)   2♠. Overjoyed but not overhasty.

      (c)   2NT, balanced and positive.

3.   (a)   3◇, showing your suit.

      (b)   2NT, protecting your kings. After a Benjamin 2♣ open-
              ing, the 2NT and 3NT rebids imply a long minor rather
              than balanced shape.

      (c)   3♣. Shows this type of hand. Partner will bid one more
              with a likely trick (e.g. a king or an outside singleton).

4.   (a)   3♠. Show your suit.

      (b)   3♠. The club fit can wait while you show your major.

      (c)   4NT, Blackwood. Your diamond suit should provide all
              the discards partner needs so if partner shows two aces,
              bid 7♣, or if partner shows one ace, try 6♣.

PLAY HANDS — THE BENJAMIN 2♣

HAND 9   DLR: North   VUL: EW

Game after a negative - anticipating and disposing of losers

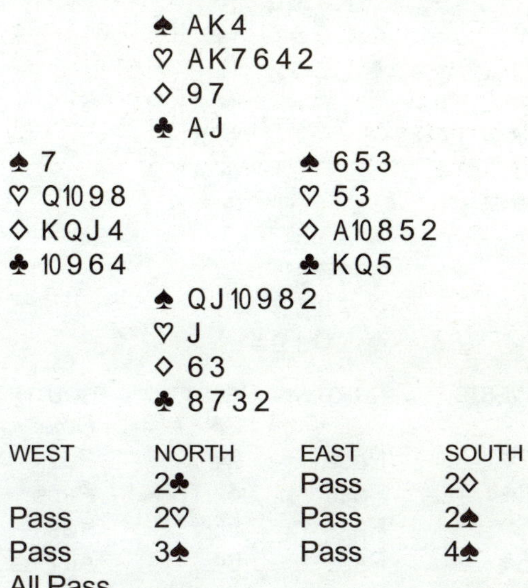

WEST	NORTH	EAST	SOUTH
	2♣	Pass	2◇
Pass	2♡	Pass	2♠
Pass	3♠	Pass	4♠
All Pass			

The bidding: South shows a negative but is worth a bid of 2♠ on the next round, and the game is reached.

Lead: ◇K.

The play: The defence cashes two top diamonds then switches to clubs, won by dummy's ace. Drawing trumps now will leave South with too many low clubs to dispose of. By postponing trumps, declarer could ruff a club in dummy and make the contract.

But there is a better line: if hearts break 3-3 or 4-2, they can be set up for an overtrick. On this line too, you can't rush trumps - dummy's ♠AK are needed as entries. Play ♡A, ruff a heart (high), lead ♠2 to ♠A, ruff a heart, then play two more rounds of trumps *finishing in dummy*. Now cash ♡K76, discarding your clubs.

HAND 10   DLR: East   VUL: Both

Slam after fit is found - setting up a long suit - finessing

```
                    ♠ 3 2
                    ♥ K J 10 9
                    ◊ Q 9 8
                    ♣ 10 8 3 2
      ♠ Q J 10                    ♠ A K 9 8 7 6 5
      ♥ A Q 7 6 2                 ♥ 5
      ◊ J 10 4                    ◊ A K 2
      ♣ 7 6                       ♣ A 5
                    ♠ 4
                    ♥ 8 4 3
                    ◊ 7 6 5 3
                    ♣ K Q J 9 4
```

WEST	NORTH	EAST	SOUTH
		2♣	Dble
2♥	Pass	2♠	Pass
3♠	Pass	4NT	Pass
5◊	Pass	5NT	Pass
6♣	Pass	6♠	All Pass

The bidding: East has over nine tricks. When partner shows a positive plus spade fit, it's only a question of whether to bid 6♠ or 7♠. West's unhelpful response when asked for kings settles the issue. South's double of an artificial bid (2♣) shows that suit.

Lead: ♣K.

The play: Declarer has a club loser and a possible diamond loser. Rather than stake all on a red suit finesse it is better to try to set up a trick in hearts; if that doesn't work, you won't have lost a trick in the process so there will still be time to try the diamond finesse.

All dummy's entries will be needed, so don't waste time. Play ♥A and ruff a heart, cross to dummy with a trump and ruff a heart, cross to dummy again and ruff another heart. Cross back to dummy and cash ♥Q, throwing the club loser. If you now try the diamond finesse you wIll discover this is your lucky day - making seven.

HAND 11   DLR: South   VUL: Nil

Opting for 3NT - Ducking to maintain an entry

```
                    ♠ A Q 7 5 3 2
                    ♡ A Q
                    ♢ A Q
                    ♣ K 6 4
   ♠ J 10 6 4                      ♠ K 9 8
   ♡ 8 6 3                         ♡ K J 10 4
   ♢ K 4 2                         ♢ J 10 9 8 3
   ♣ Q 9 7                         ♣ 8
                    ♠ —
                    ♡ 9 7 5 2
                    ♢ 7 6 5
                    ♣ A J 10 5 3 2
```

WEST	NORTH	EAST	SOUTH
			Pass
Pass	2♣	Pass	2♢
Pass	2♠	Pass	3♣
Pass	3NT	All Pass	

The bidding: North has a fit with clubs, but 3NT is the likely game and by bidding it, North's AQ holdings are protected if the opening lead is in one of those suits.

Lead: ♢J.

The play: The long club suit is needed to bring home this contract and as there are no entries to dummy in the other suits, ♣A will need to be carefully preserved. Cash ♣K and play another club. West shows out so declarer knows a club trick will have to be given up. Do it now, keeping ♣A as an entry so the clubs aren't stranded!

HAND 12   DLR:West   VUL: NS

Game after a negative - ruffing finesse

```
                        ♠ 6 4 2
                        ♡ K 6 5 3 2
                        ◇ K Q J
                        ♣ Q 3
        ♠ A K J 10 9 5              ♠ Q 8 7
        ♡ A                         ♡ Q J 9 4
        ◇ A 8 6                     ◇ 7 5 2
        ♣ A 9 5                     ♣ 7 4 2
                        ♠ 3
                        ♡ 10 8 7
                        ◇ 10 9 4 3
                        ♣ K J 10 8 6
```

WEST	NORTH	EAST	SOUTH
2♣	Pass	2◇	Pass
2♠	Pass	3♠	Pass
4♠	All pass		

The bidding: East shows a fit and invites game. West accepts.

Lead: ◇K.

The play: There are four losers looming ominously for declarer in those flat minor suits, so at least one of them must be discarded on dummy's hearts if this contract is to be bagged. After winning ◇A, cash just one round of trumps with ♠A (dummy's ♠Q8 will be needed later as entries), then unblock ♡A so that the stage is set to cross to dummy and set up hearts.

Play ♠5 over to dummy's ♠8, then lead ♡Q for a ruffing finesse. It does not matter that the finesse loses because a diamond is thrown away on it anyway (loser on loser). North can cash one diamond trick, but declarer will win the next lead, cross to dummy with ♠Q, and throw a club on the ♡J. Noting the fall of ♡10, declarer cashes ♡9, discarding the other club loser. Making 11 tricks.

Glossary

Term	Explanation
Acol Two Bid	an opening bid of 2◇/♡/♠ in the Acol system, showing that suit and at least eight playing tricks
artificial	call that is not natural
balanced hand	hand with no singleton or void, and at most one doubleton
Benjamin Twos	convention incorporating strong & weak twos
Blackwood	a bid of 4NT asking how many aces partner has (5♣=0 or 4, 5◇=1, 5♡=2, 5♠=3), optionally followed by 5NT to ask for kings
cheapest suit	the suit that keeps the bidding lowest, also called "bidding up the line"
cue bid	a bid of the enemy suit (forcing). Can also refer to the bidding of controls in a slam auction
defensive	defensive tricks are likely winners if defending the opponents' contract, as distinct from *offensive* or *playing* tricks
ducking	playing low from both hands, in order to preserve an entry
entry	card used to get to a particular hand
fast arrival	the principle that in a game forcing auction, jumping straight to game is weaker than raising partner's suit below game
favourable	favourable vulnerability is when you are not vulnerable and the opponents are vulnerable
finesse	attempt to win with lower-ranked card(s), based on the position of the missing big card(s)
fit	at least eight cards in a suit between the two hands, advisable for trumps
forcing	a call that partner may not pass
fourth seat	position of the fourth player to call
gambling 3NT	opening 3NT based on a long, solid minor
game forcing	situation where the partnership is committed to continue bidding until game is reached
HCP	high card points (A=4, K=3, Q=2, J=1)
honours	aces, kings, queens, jacks and tens

invite	ask partner to bid on unless minimum
jump	a bid at a level higher than necessary; e.g. over 1♡, a bid of 2♠ or 3♡
loser	a card that is expected to lose to the opponents if the suit is led
marked finesse	a finesse that is sure to work, usually because one opponent already showed out so the other opponent is known to hold the missing cards in that suit
Michaels Cue Bid	conventional bid of the enemy suit to show a 2-suiter
natural	call that "means what it says"
negative	artificial call to show weakness. In answer to a Benjamin 2♣ or 2♢, the next suit up is negative and indicates 0-7 HCP
Ogust	2NT enquiry in response to a weak two, asking the weak two bidder to describe the hand strength and suit quality
overcall	first bid by the side that did not open
overtake	play a higher card over partner's high card, to "get to where you want to be"
passout seat	the position in which passing would conclude the auction. The player in this position may sometimes call with below normal strength, to prevent the bidding from ending
playing tricks	offensive tricks, likely to be made if that player's long suit becomes trumps
positive	constructive response in a forcing situation. In response to a Benjamin 2♣ or 2♢, a positive shows 8+ HCP
Precision	system that opens 1♣ with 16+ HCP
pre-empt	weak, high bid, primarily obstructive
quick tricks	A=1, AK=2, AQ=1½, KQ=1, Kx=½
rebid	a rebid is a player's second bid; to rebid a suit is to bid the same suit a second time
ruffing finesse	involves leading from a run of honours when holding a void opposite, so that if the second player has the higher honour, it can be ruffed

sacrifice	bidding something not to make, but to stop the opponents making their contract
sequence	touching cards (headed by an honour)
short hand	usually refers to the hand (out of declarer and dummy) with fewer trumps
shortage pts (SP)	point count used to value short suits after a fit is found: void=5, singleton=3, doubleton=1
slam	bid of six (small slam) or seven (grand slam)
Stayman	convention asking partner to bid a 4-card major. Only applies when partner has bid notrumps as the first natural call for our side
stopper	holding which is likely to stop the opponents running a suit, e.g. A, Kx, Qxx, Jxxx or better
system	set of agreements on the meanings of bids
takeout double	use of a double to ask partner to bid
third seat	position of third player to call (partner of dealer)
tolerance	reasonable support only, e.g. doubleton opposite partner's long suit, or 3-card support for a suit of which partner may have only four
total points (TP)	HCP + shortage points
transfer	artificial bid showing 5+ cards, usually in the next suit up
unbalanced	hands with a singleton or void. When used in a non-specific way, the term may encompass semi-balanced hands (hands with no singleton or void, but with more than one doubleton)
unblock	play out high card(s) from the shorter holding, to facilitate entry to the longer holding in a suit (to avoid being "stuck in the wrong hand")
unusual 2NT	generally played only as an overcall, it shows a 2-suiter, normally a weak hand with 5-5 in the minors (partner is expected to bid one of these suits). Occasionally the "unusual notrump" can apply at other levels, e.g. 4NT
weak twos	show about 6-10 HCP, 6-card suit. Playing Benjamin Twos, 2♥ or 2♠ are weak two openings
yarborough	hand containing no honours

(1) N/Nil
♠ K Q 9 6 5 4
♥ Q J 4
♦ 6 5 3
♣ J

(2) E/NS
♠ K 10 4 3 2
♥ 10
♦ 10 8 4 3
♣ Q 8 5

(3) S/EW
♠ K 9 4
♥ A K Q J 9
♦ A 5 4 2
♣ 10

(4) W/Both
♠ 7 6 4
♥ A 3
♦ Q J 9 2
♣ Q J 10 9

(5) N/NS
♠ K J 9 7
♥ A Q J
♦ A 3
♣ A K J 9

(6) E/EW
♠ Q 5 4 3
♥ 10
♦ K 5 3
♣ K 8 7 4 3

(7) S/Both
♠ 9 7 4 2
♥ 8
♦ A 5 4
♣ 8 7 5 4 2

(8) W/Nil
♠ 7 6 5
♥ Q J 10 8 6
♦ 7
♣ J 9 8 6

(9) N/EW
♠ A K 4
♥ A K 7 6 4 2
♦ 9 7
♣ A J

(10) E/Both
♠ 3 2
♥ K J 10 9
♦ Q 9 8
♣ 10 8 3 2

(11) S/Nil
♠ A Q 7 5 3 2
♥ A Q
♦ A Q
♣ K 6 4

(12) W/NS
♠ 6 4 2
♥ K 6 5 3 2
♦ K Q J
♣ Q 3

SOUTH HANDS

(1) N/Nil
♠ A J 7 3
♥ —
♦ A J 10 9 4
♣ 10 7 6 2

(2) E/NS
♠ A Q 5
♥ 8 4 3
♦ K Q J
♣ 10 9 4 3

(3) S/EW
♠ A Q 10 8 3 2
♥ 10 5 3
♦ 10 6 3
♣ J

(4) W/Both
♠ A 3 2
♥ Q J 5
♦ 8 7 6 5
♣ A 5 3

(5) N/NS
♠ 8 6 3
♥ 10 8 4
♦ 6 4
♣ Q 10 7 6 2

(6) E/EW
♠ 8 6
♥ 9 8
♦ Q 10 9 8 4
♣ J 10 9 2

(7) S/Both
♠ A K Q 10 3
♥ A K
♦ 10
♣ A K Q 10 6

(8) W/Nil
♠ A Q 10 2
♥ 5 4
♦ J 6 5 3
♣ 4 3 2

(9) N/EW
♠ Q J 10 9 8 2
♥ J
♦ 6 3
♣ 8 7 3 2

(10) E/Both
♠ 4
♥ 8 4 3
♦ 7 6 5 3
♣ K Q J 9 4

(11) S/Nil
♠ —
♥ 9 7 5 2
♦ 7 6 5
♣ A J 10 5 3 2

(12) W/NS
♠ 3
♥ 10 8 7
♦ 10 9 4 3
♣ K J 10 8 6

(1) N/Nil
♠ 10
♡ A K 5 3 2
♢ Q 7
♣ Q 9 5 4 3

(2) E/NS
♠ 9 7
♡ Q 9 2
♢ A 9 7 2
♣ A K 7 6

(3) S/EW
♠ J 7 6 5
♡ 8 6
♢ K Q
♣ A 9 7 5 4

(4) W/Both
♠ K Q 10 9 8 5
♡ 10 2
♢ K 10 3
♣ 8 6

(5) N/NS
♠ 10 5 2
♡ K 7 5 2
♢ K 10 8 7 2
♣ 3

(6) E/EW
♠ J 10 9 7 2
♡ A 7 6
♢ J 7 2
♣ Q 6

(7) S/Both
♠ —
♡ Q 6 5 3 2
♢ Q J 9 6 3 2
♣ J 9

(8) W/Nil
♠ K J 9 4 3
♡ A K
♢ A Q
♣ A K 10 5

(9) N/EW
♠ 7
♡ Q 10 9 8
♢ K Q J 4
♣ 10 9 6 4

(10) E/Both
♠ Q J 10
♡ A Q 7 6 2
♢ J 10 4
♣ 7 6

(11) S/Nil
♠ J 10 6 4
♡ 8 6 3
♢ K 4 2
♣ Q 9 7

(12) W/NS
♠ A K J 10 9 5
♡ A
♢ A 8 6
♣ A 9 5

EAST HANDS

(1) N/Nil
♠ 8 2
♡ 10 9 8 7 6
♢ K 8 2
♣ A K 8

(2) E/NS
♠ J 8 6
♡ A K J 7 6 5
♢ 6 5
♣ J 2

(3) S/EW
♠ —
♡ 7 4 2
♢ J 9 8 7
♣ K Q 8 6 3 2

(4) W/Both
♠ J
♡ K 9 8 7 6 4
♢ A 4
♣ K 7 4 2

(5) N/NS
♠ A Q 4
♡ 9 6 3
♢ Q J 9 5
♣ 8 5 4

(6) E/EW
♠ A K
♡ K Q J 5 4 3 2
♢ A 6
♣ A 5

(7) S/Both
♠ J 8 6 5
♡ J 10 9 7 4
♢ K 8 7
♣ 3

(8) W/Nil
♠ 8
♡ 9 7 3 2
♢ K 10 9 8 4 2
♣ Q 7

(9) N/EW
♠ 6 5 3
♡ 5 3
♢ A 10 8 5 2
♣ K Q 5

(10) E/Both
♠ A K 9 8 7 6 5
♡ 5
♢ A K 2
♣ A 5

(11) S/Nil
♠ K 9 8
♡ K J 10 4
♢ J 10 9 8 3
♣ 8

(12) W/NS
♠ Q 8 7
♡ Q J 9 4
♢ 7 5 2
♣ 7 4 2